The Greedy King

Written by Jane Wood

Illustrated by Graham Philpot

There was once a very greedy king. He owned all the land that he could see, but he wanted more.

"I want more land!" he shouted. "More, more, MORE!"

Next to the king's land there was another country where many people lived. The king wanted their land for himself.

He took his men to tell
the people to leave
their land.

"The king wants
your land," said the men.
"You have to get out – NOW!"

4

"Where can we go? What can we do?
How can we live without our land?"
the people asked.

The greedy king didn't care
what happened to the people.
He just wanted their land.

A little girl came to see the king.
"Please sir," she said, "I have
an idea. I can give you something
much better than this land.

"I can give you something that no one else has ever seen before. If I give it to you, will you let us keep our land?"

The king was very surprised.
What could there be that no one
had ever seen before? Whatever it was,
he had to have it.

"Very well," he said at last. "Bring it
to me. If no one has ever seen it before,
I will let you keep your land."

The next day the little girl came
to the palace. She was carrying
a small basket.

"What have you got for me?"
asked the king.

The little girl put her hand in
the basket. Carefully, she took out...

... an egg. An ordinary, smooth, brown egg.

"An egg?" screamed the king.
"Everyone in the world has seen an egg!
You lose! I keep the land!"

"Just wait," said the little girl.

Soon, the egg began to move.

Then it began to crack.

Then at last, out hopped...

... a chick, a brand new little chick
that no one had ever seen before.

"I win," said the little girl.
"We keep our land."